PANDEMIC POEMS OF 2020

"If the Cholera or black plague should come to these shores, perhaps the bulk of the nation would pray to be delivered from it, but the rest would put their trust in the Health Board."

-Mark Twain

PANDEMIC POEMS OF 2020

JIM KINTNER

©2020 Jim Kintner

All rights reserved. No part of this book may be used or reproduced in any manner whatsoever without the prior written consent of the author. All newspaper headlines in this book are non-copy righted excerpts.

ISBN: 978-0-578-73729-4

This book is dedicated

to the First Responders

who have saved so many lives

...

Introduction

•••

The poems in this book, "Pandemic Poems of 2020" were written during the Covid-19 Pandemic from March 12th to August 12th, 2020. The newspaper headlines adjacent to each poem represent the newspaper headlines on the day that each poem was written. I have selected newspaper headlines from different newspapers across the United States. There is no doubt that the hours of boredom sheltered at home contributed to the subject matters of the poems written. This year has thrust home schooling, zoom meetings, shopping with masks and gloves, and isolation onto all of us. My goal in writing these poems is to provide some levity, empathy, and reflection on the magnitude of the effects of the pandemic on everyone. It is indeed a global event that has changed the world. I hope you enjoy reading them as much as I enjoyed writing them.

Jim Kintner
Indio, California
August 2020

TABLE OF CONTENTS

POEMS

1. Trapped at Home -------------------------------- 13
2. Time to Work -------------------------------------- 15
3. The Longest Month ----------------------------- 17
4. Against All Odds --------------------------------- 19
5. Sink or Swim ------------------------------------- 21
6. Mixed Signals ------------------------------------ 23
7. Social Distancing -------------------------------- 25
8. The Limits --- 27
9. Surviving and Thriving ------------------------- 29
10. Angels of Mercy --------------------------------- 31
11. The CDC Way ------------------------------------- 33
12. In the ICU --- 35
13. To Open or Not ---------------------------------- 37
14. Stir Crazy -- 39
15. The Jolt of Covid-19 ---------------------------- 41
16. Don't Listen to Stupid ------------------------- 43
17. The Fact of the Matter ----------------------- 45
18. For Better or Worse --------------------------- 47
19. It's Great to be Alive -------------------------- 49
20. Waiting for Relief ------------------------------- 51
21. In Total Disbelief -------------------------------- 53
22. What's Next -------------------------------------- 55
23. Surviving 2020 ----------------------------------- 57

24. Just the Way It Is	59
25. Someone Else's Problem	61
26. Wall Street Blues	63
27. What Day Is It?	65
28. What's Ahead?	67
29. What Could Have Been	69
30. Feels Like A Dream-	71
31. Looked Down Again	73
32. Mixed Messages	75
33. A Day At Camp	77
34. Pandemic Hallucinations	79
35. What Went Wrong?	81
36. Dr. Fauci Fired	83
37. Locked Up Again	85
38. It's Not A Hoax	87
39. Saying No To Masks	89
40. Real or Not Real	91
41. The Vaccine	93
42. The Status Quo	95
43. Staying the Course	97
44. Sorry Isn't Enough	99
45. Stay Worry Free	101
46. Happy is the Way	103
47. How Weird Can It Get?	105
48. The Truth About Masks	107
49. Failure to Pitch In	109
50. Frozen in Time	111
CDC COVID-19 Guidelines	113

"STATEWIDE STAY AT HOME ORDER IN CALIFORNIA"

"CORONAVIRUS IN ALL FIFTY STATES"

-The Washington Post
March 17th, 2020

TRAPPED AT HOME

A person's home is his or her castle,
Getting out and about, sometimes is a hassle.
Shopping for groceries, putting gas in the car,
All necessary things if you want to eat and go far.

A Dailey routine, often work, sleep, and eat,
Sometimes called a rut, that you do not want to repeat.
But free will gives everyone the right of choice,
Deciding what is exciting when it is time to rejoice.

At the present time, all that is gone,
Social isolation the norm from dawn to dawn.
Reading books, taking a nap, or watching tv,
It is week after week of let us wait and see.

The future of our country's now at risk,
The edict passed; now daily instructions given on a computer disk.
Lock down is next, mostly in a big city,
Soon "trapped at home" mandated, we are not sitting so pretty.

"STRANDED BY THE CORONAVIRUS"

"TECH HEADACHES FROM WORKING FROM HOME"

-The New York Times
March 19th, 2020

TIME TO WORK

The "Quarantine Lockdown", is not a joke,
Extra time for chores, the wife's list to evoke.
Painting the bathroom, mopping the floors,
Perhaps trimming the edge of a stuck door.

Pulling weeds in the back yard,
Washing the car, not too hard.
For those living in an old house,
Cleaning the attic, perhaps meeting a mouse.

Remodeling the kitchen, new appliances and more,
Not for everyone, just handy men to the core.
New LED lights overhead, saving lots of money,
New tile on the floor, requested by my honey.

Staying busy will keep us sane,
But do not ever forget your golf game.
Now seeing 2020, our vision is now clear,
The virus will end, nothing more to fear.

"CALIFORNIA SMASHES THE DAILY CASE RECORD"

"MEN IN ORANGE COUNTY DON'T WEAR MASKS"

-The Los Angeles Times
March 29th, 2020

THE LONGEST MONTH

The longest month, March, the third of this year,
Only thirty-one days long, it has brought no cheer.
A pandemic, a recession, and a quarantine,
Unbelievable events, like we have never seen.

A toilet paper shortage, brought on so quick,
Now bathroom duties are now quite a trick.
Food shelves are bare at the grocery store,
Panicking shoppers now hungry looking for more.

Businesses shut down, no restaurants or bars,
Golf courses closed too, no birdies or pars.
The future unclear, now hoping for the best,
Wondering who came up with this ridiculous test.

The news coverage hourly, continues to be grim,
Trying to stay fit walking, but not in the gym.
Taking our time until April Fool's Day,
Praying for relief, maybe soon being able to go outside and play.

"FLORIDA, SOUTH CAROLINA, GEORGIA, TEXAS EASE RESTRICTIONS"

"TRUMP CLAIMS CORORNAVIRUS TESTS ARE WIDELY AVAILABLE"

    -The USA Today
      April 22nd, 2020

AGAINST THE ODDS

Bookies and Doctors, always set the odds,
A game of chance or a life, beating the spread, maybe an act of God.
As we face the pandemic across 50 states,
Opening America, still up for debate.

Oil the lowest price in twenty years,
The economy now weak, time to change gears.
Food banks near empty, time to go back to work,
What is worse, being broke or going berserk.

Time will give us the answer, whether it is wrong,
God help us if "Amazing Grace" becomes our #1 song.
Americans have taken big risks before,
The world wars required us to open our door.

Las Vegas and Reno will set the high and low,
Will we quarantine again because we did not go slow?
If everyone masks, and stays six feet apart,
We will all stay safe and we will be ready for a new start.

"SALON RESTRICTIONS IN PLACE FOR SOCIAL DISTANCING"

"CORONAVIRUS GROW DAILY AS MASKS NOT WORN"

-Houston Chronicle
April 25th, 2020

SINK OR SWIM

The tides of humanity have been going in and out,
Good fortune followed by famine, have left us in doubt.
This pandemic another reminder of where we are,
In between wars, natural disasters, and a trip to the stars.

Every one of us is playing Russian roulette,
Each day we arise, we do not know what we will get.
Could be happiness or our last day here,
We just roll the dice living without any fear.

Keeping our country going, surviving the best we can,
It has always been that way since the start of man.
No guarantees given for tomorrow,
Cheer and joy daily, sometimes sorrow.

The up and down of life, just the way it is,
Food on the table, money made from biz.
Sink or swim, the moment of truth at hand,
Let us hope our next tune is "Strike up the Band"

SALON RESTRICTIONS IN PLACE
FOR SOCIAL DISTANCING"

"CORONAVIRUS GROW DAILY
AS MASKS NOT WORN"

-The Oklahoman
May 3rd, 2020

MIXED MESSAGES

The truth about the Coronavirus, often is skewed,
The CDC and the White House are engaged in a media feud.
The number of confirmed cases, and those that die,
Are real numbers, that leave thousands to cry,

The CDC announcing that with so many out in mass,
It will cause confirmed cases to soar; many more will pass.
Yet, the White House announced 99% will not get sick,
The danger of this contagious virus, so they say just a dirty trick.

The truth from Dr. Fauci is we are in terrible shape,
With so many violating social restrictions, a national disgrace.
The pandemic has set us back weeks and weeks,
It will not be safe to go out until the virus peaks.

The future of the country is uncertain on so many levels,
It is almost like the growing scourge is controlled by devils.
Hoping and praying that the Almighty Lord,
Helps us launch a virus free world, with everyone on board.

"3,972 CASES AND
238 DEATHS IN 39   COUNTIES"

"PANDEMIC LEADS TO
ECONOMIC DECLINE"

-The Dallas Morning News
May 6th, 2020

SOCIAL DISTANCING

Staying six feet apart, is now the new social norm,
Brought to America on by the Covid-19 storm.
FaceTime and Zoom are now the apps for viewing,
Sharing moments with loved ones and friends, in a love fest renewing.

Sometimes the boredom, can be a little too much,
Thereafter, resolving the issue with meditation, prayer, or a soothing hand to touch.
Important to remember, that millions are sheltered in,
So, the nation can survive, and declare a win-win.

Watching movies, playing cards, or reading,
The time seems to drag on, as everyone is pleading.
When can we eat out or go to a bar?
Dr. Brix says, "Just wait until the President stops acting bizarre".

The use of masks and social distancing,
Saves lives for all that are listening.
As we move into the future, we need to be smart,
And remember that the solution to this crisis, comes from the heart.

"THIRD DAY WITH NO DEATHS"

"RESTRICTIONS ARE WORKING TO REDUCE CORONAVIRUS CASES"

-The Oregonian
May 10th, 2020

THE LIMITS

The number of restrictions, now in place,
Redefine living for the human race.
Six feet apart, a mask on your face,
Rules to enforce until the virus leaves without a trace.

Now a limit on paper towels and toilet paper,
Disinfectant used everywhere, leaving a chemical vapor.
A meat shortage threatens beef eaters,
As shoppers in stores are limited by greeters.

There's no Clorox, Purell, or other germ killers,
No Gloves and masks, building drama like Stephen King thrillers.
As our new world emerges, out of the stay in place rules,
The kids stuck learning at home, with the closure of schools.

It is totally scary as business starts to resume,
The anxiety builds, as the number of deceased bring gloom.
So much to think about during the pandemic,
As we pray for a resolution, to a virus pandemic that is so systemic.

"THE GRAND THEATRE CUTS 60% OF ITS STAFF"

"CORONAVIRUS CRIPPLES INDUSTRY"

-The Wilmington News-Journal
May 12th, 2020

SURVIVING and THRIVING

The challenge of staying well during the pandemic,
A truly daunting experience, not just academic.
At the same time trying to be productive,
Trying to get a positive result, without be conductive.

It is staying in the house, working from home,
So tired of inactivity, hours maybe being alone.
The lack of interaction with good friends,
Any person contact precluded until the virus risk ends.

What does it take to feel fulfilled?
When the daily gauntlet is thrust to construct or build.
To do something special or spectacular,
Or something "Out of this world", in the common vernacular.

There is no choice when survival's at stake,
Forging on the only thought, needing luck and a good break.
If it is possible to thrive, and do something good,
The results reviewed later of this time, will stand out and be understood.

"TALKING CAN GENERATE COVID-19 DROPLETS"

"COVID-19 CASES FILL HOSPITALS"

-The Hartford Courant
May 14th, 2020

ANGELS OF MERCY

The Covid-19 Virus pandemic is now like a plague,
So contagious and deadly, yet unknown and vague.
With the country overwhelmed with new cases,
Hospitals, doctors, and nurses, daily treating new faces.

So random the effects of this new threat,
Some cases are mild, the affected, barely breaking a sweat.
Others not so lucky, out of breath,
Without a ventilator, they are marked for death.

The angels of mercy, gather for the fight,
Lives to save, their duty, to heal and care into the night.
PPE's needed for them to stay well,
Doubters and haters need to go to hell.

The time of concern is now upon us,
Stay at home directives, must be maintained, without a fuss.
No second chances maybe afforded,
Obeying the rules, lives saved, families rewarded.

"COVID-19 CASES RISE AT AN ALARMING RATE"

"HOSPITAL BEDS FILLED"

-The Los Angeles Times
May 15th, 2020

IN THE ICU

There is a place you do not want to go,
It is in the hospital, the ICU, where each minute goes slow.
A special wing, built just to help the seriously sick,
Modern medicine the cure, trying to do the trick.

The Covid-19 virus, the enemy, vicious and mean,
So lethal at times, the only deterrent is quarantine.
The grim reaper waits for some without luck,
Others on ventilators, intubated and awestruck.

The doctors and nurses in the ICU are working overtime,
They are risking their lives for others, should be crime.
It is their job in the ICU to save lives,
Patients are more than statistics, stored in the archives.

It is life or death each and every day,
Beating the virus, the only mission, any conceivable way.
The dedication and training make them heroes,
Striving to get Covid-19 deaths down to triple zeroes.

"PHILADELPHIA ENFORCES CDC RESTRICTIONS"

"COVID-19 CASES RISING"

-The Philadelphia Inquirer
May 15th, 2020

THE CDC WAY

New Covid-19 guidelines released by the CDC,
To open the country, from shutdown to being free.
These steps are based on science, to keep us well,
Not a contrived hoax, or a show and tell.

Keeping people safe from this horrible disease,
Appealing to a person's reason, beginning with please.
Social distancing and take out, until the numbers go down,
Wearing a mask when near others, without a frown.

No bars or restaurants, where people like to mingle,
Six feet apart at the store, in a line that is single.
Gloves on at the gas pump, when filling up,
Wash your hands often, drink from a clean cup.

Essential travel only, do not press your luck,
Being inconsiderate towards others, you will be called a schmuck.
America's Bill of Rights does not cover hurting others,
Protecting each other, a must, acting like sisters and brothers.

"COVID19 CURVE MUST BE SMOOSHED"

"GOVENOR CUOMO ISSUES PHASES TO RE-OPEN"

    -The Buffalo News
       May 16th, 2020

TO OPEN OR NOT

The weeks under quarantine, totally distressing,
The fear of going out to a bar, equally stressing.
The President says it is totally safe,
"Its Fake News" as we all know is really unsafe.

Who do you trust during the shut-down?
To find any safe place anywhere in town.
Does someone have a crystal ball?
The right answer somewhere, "Need to Call Saul!"

Maybe a Tarot Cards Reader, or some Psychics,
Voodoo maybe the answer, just for kicks.
A life or death risk, now being downplayed,
The economy always more important when somebody gets paid.

Smart money will just stay home,
Talking to friends just on the phone,
The dangerous virus is still out there,
Until there are no new cases, stay put, it could be anywhere.

"GREEN COUNTY JAIL REPORTS COVID-19 CASES"

"SUBSTITUTE TEACHERS AT RISK DUE TO COVID-19 CASES"

-The Springfield News-Leader
May 17th, 2020

STIR CRAZY

Like being locked up in prison, for breaking the law,
In a ten by ten cell, impossible to withdraw,
Now stuck at home, just to stay well,
Not wanting to leave too soon for either Heaven or hell.

A new mental state develops called "Stir Crazy",
The condition arises when your vision gets hazy.
Only so much TV, reading books, or more,
Gin Rummy not fun when you do not keep score.

The same routine, everything the same way,
It is similar to the script in "Ground hog Day".
Over and over, three meals affecting my weight,
As a special bonus, a one-year diet awaits.

The ultimate benefit of being a shut in,
The only relief to this syndrome comes from drinking gin.
Hoping for a miracle to end this nightmare,
The vaccine the only choice, to end this pandemic scare.

"VIRUS SCIENTIST'S NEWS ON COVID 19 SKEWED"

"LISTENERS SKEPTICAL ABOUT COVID-19 CASES"

-The Indianapolis Recorder
May 20th, 2020

THE JOLT OF COVID-19

It is not the flu, it is much worse,
The virus's symptoms arrive like a curse.
Starts with a cough, sore throat, and fever,
Out of nowhere, the loss of breath, makes you a believer.

It is Russian Roulette, and the Lottery, all in one,
The losers get sick, and maybe their lives are done,
No one plans on meeting their maker,
When the day comes it is a life breaker.

So Covid-19 can just arrive at your door,
Brought in on anything, like glitter on the floor.
A feature of any microbe, is it is deadly and small,
And It is so persistent, it sticks around for the long haul.

Like a lightning bolt from a thunderstorm,
It brought a pandemic, the world now demanding major health reform.
The jolt to all of us, a life changing event,
Everyone now hating this contagious virus, we will hereafter work hard to prevent

"TEENS SPREAD VIRUS WITH 'PARTY ZERO' MENTALITY"

"GREENWICH VOWS TO ENFORCE RESPTRICTIONS"

-Greenwich Time
May 24th, 2020

DON'T LISTEN TO STUPID

As the Sunshine States opened up,
The beaches are now full, the virus is bound to show up.
Dr. Brix warned that things could get much worse,
Those doubting her words, may leave in a hearse.

Cries from some heard were "We can do whatever we please!",
The quarantine orders were to stay put, and just freeze.
Defying the law and medical science,
So many in violation of the rules of compliance.

The wisdom imparted by our leading experts,
Is meant to prevent the virus's death spurts.
Too many zealous idiots ignoring social distancing,
For a second in the spotlight, perhaps to gain financial positioning.

So please, "Don't Listen to Stupid", when invited to party,
Remember the risks, pledge to staying hale and hearty.
It is an extremely dangerous time to just go out,
Out of nowhere the virus could come, bringing a permanent knock out.

"STATEWIDE MASK ORDER"

"COVID-19 HOSPITALIZATIONS ARE DOWN"

-The Denver Post
May 14th, 2020

THE FACT OF THE MATTER

After ninety days stuck in the house,
Home schooling the kids, no time to grouse.
Boutiques are closed, hair salons too,
All beauty secrets gone; some start to feel blue.

The walls of the house start to close in,
Eating too much, impossible to stay thin.
The cocktail hour starts earlier each day,
A good excuse to send the kids out to play.

Sanity is a subject we cannot talk about,
Summer vacations now in doubt.
It is a strange time in the U.S.A.,
No solution to the virus in sight, but some say it is okay.

The summer of 2020, will test us all,
Hoping for a vaccine in the early Fall.
We are open for business, come what may,
The strength of the nation, tested, but we will find a way.

"CASINOS STAY SHUT DURING PANDEMIC"

"ECONOMY SUFFERS FROM COVID-19 PANDEMIC"

-The Las Vegas Sun
May 28th, 2020

FOR BETTER OR WORSE

The adage, "It takes a village", is so unique,
As America was shut down, the majority started to freak.
In New York, with orders still in place,
Businesses opened in revolt, no disgrace.

The entrepreneur's movement to defy the law,
By necessity to avoid bankruptcy, each one now an outlaw.
The fear of death, now just words,
The respect for the shut-down, for the birds.

The Covid-19 pandemic has raged on,
The numbers growing, regret for those gone.
The instinct of survival, now takes over,
Ninety days shut, the end, a capitalist takeover.

For better or worse, our country must carry on,
Riding out this plague, rebuilding, forgetting what is gone.
The world has changed in 2020,
The choice made, the loss of a few, for the good of the many.

"SOCIAL GATHERINGS RESTRICTED"

"AIR RESTRICTIONS TO TEXAS LIFTED"

-The El Paso Weekly
May 28th, 2020

IT'S GREAT TO BE ALIVE

As we live through the Covid-19 pandemic,
The reason to stay well, is not just academic.
Regardless of age, each year is irreplaceable,
The experiences in life, priceless, ever so embraceable.

The threat of getting sick, and maybe dying,
Just a nightmare, unnerving and emotional trying.
So, staying safe, wearing a mask, and sheltering in,
The smartest things to do, to avoid being a "has been".

Rejoicing in living, being totally alive,
Breathing in and out, listening to Dave Brubeck play "Take Five".
A moment of silence, to honor a loved one,
Waking up early at dawn, to see the rising sun.

Ten thousand reasons to not take a risk,
Running, biking, or sailing into a wind that is brisk.
"It's great to be alive", words to live by,
Delaying the trip to the sweet "By and By".

"TESTING CAPACITY EXPANDED FOR COVID-19"

"ECONOMY SUFFERS FROM PANDEMIC"

-San Francisco Examiner
May 31st, 2020

WAITING FOR RELIEF

The promise of tomorrow rests on good news,
A stop to the virus, no more singing the blues,
After days of being sheltered, the household repairs now all fixed,
The cure of the virus unknown, scientific opinions daily are mixed.

Conflicting views posted claiming it is a hoax,
Apparently, the doubters do not care about the old folks.
Sheltering in place should be nationwide,
However, some Governors are foolish, their states will soon be on the downside.

Day after day, more time on our hands,
No restaurants or bars featuring live bands.
Creative cooking, games of checkers or chess,
Time off without pay, financial recovery now just a guess.

Trapped in a time lock, almost like Marshall Law,
Imposed globally to save Grandma and Grandpa.
Praying for relief, the date now in the God's Hand,
When that day comes, life will again be grand.

"CHANGE INFLICTED BY COVID-19"

"TOURISM HIT BY LOCKDOWN"

-The Desert Sun
June 5th, 2020

IN TOTAL DISBELIEF

As the weeks pass, and the numbers keep going up,
Projections of fewer cases, just a cover-up.
Impossible now with riots everywhere,
Thousands marching and protesting without masks or a care.

How can it be that so many have failed to understand?
That Covid-19 is contagious and lethal, throughout our land.
It is not going away, anytime soon,
A threat to all, no one is immune.

A vaccine is in the works, with thousands in trials,
Yet, caution is urged, testing needed for all personal profiles.
The pandemic will continue without contact tracing,
Nothing will stop the virus; it will continue racing.
The promise of the future, perhaps in question,
Political confusion, racism raging, maybe a depression.
The American people in total disbelief,
Hoping for recovery, and the end of grief.

"BUSINESS OWNERS CLAIM SIGNIFICANT LOSSES FROM PANDEMIC"

"BUSINESS OWNERS PLOT THEIR FUTURE"

-The Fort Worth Weekly
June 6th, 2020

WHAT'S NEXT

As the summer months roll on out,
Things open up, a heat wave, time to shout.
PGA Golf, NBA, and NHL hockey,
Horse racing with a masked jockey.

Restaurants, bars, and beaches now open,
Restrictions in place, relief coming, everyone hope'n.
It is not the world we used to know,
Social distancing required, everywhere you go.

Baseball games without fans in place,
TV rating the highest ever, Space X launching men into space.
Unemployment numbers higher than high,
Losses and closed businesses reaching the sky.

Fear of a second wave, now ever present,
Dr. Fauci's cautious advice, given to all, deaths to prevent.
Millions are not listening, nor taking heed,
Please, "Take the Doctor's Advice", do not let the virus succeed.

"PUBLIC PANIC AND MEDIA SCORN RISE"

"CLORAX SALES SOAR DURING PANDEMIC"

-The Wall Street Journal
June 7th, 2020

SURVIVING 2020

The year 2020, just 365 days,
Yet so different than every other, in so many ways.
Reflecting now almost half-way through, it has been surreal,
The Coronavirus killing so many, for them very real.

Quarantined to home for ninety days,
Scared of contracting the virus, still a frightening phase.
Masks, gloves, disinfectant the norm,
Like a health hurricane, a plague filled storm.

The blame for the crisis, on someone in China,
Infecting over one million, from the west coast to South Carolina.
Present in all fifty states, it rages on,
The drama continuing until we have a vaccine, and the menace is gone.

No one is absolutely safe from this plague,
Drugs mentioned for treatment, their effectiveness unusually vague.
Surviving 2020 will definitely take some luck,
Celebrating on New Year's Eve 2020, totally awestruck.

"102-YEAR-OLD WOMAN BATTLES COVID-19"

"HOSPITAL OVERWHELMED WITH COVID CASES"

-The Providence Journal
June 9th, 2020

JUST THE WAY IT IS

As the nation opens, masks in place,
Codvid-19 cases rise, blamed on the irrational rat race.
Totally unfortunate for those that get sick,
Some saying, "Business as Usual", just part of the economic yardstick.

Rolling the dice for a night on the town,
Not too intelligent, if it takes you down.
Caution for some not part of their game,
Go for the gold, maybe finding some fame.

Reckless, selfish, careless, hurting others,
Spreading the virus, to mothers, sisters, and brothers.
The anger exhibited, with restrictions enforced,
Human nature on steroids, civility and mentality divorced.

The strangest times, that we will ever see,
People protesting without masks, shouting "We're free".
The end result of this irresponsible behavior,
More innocents dying, meeting their savior.

"AN EXPLOSION OF COVID-19 CASES"

"PARTY GOERS SPREAD VIRUS"

-The Los Angeles Times
June 11th, 2020

SOMEONE ELSE'S PROBLEM

As the number of Covid-19 cases seem to surge,
The public health official's warnings seemed to just submerge.
The past projections that the pandemic could get worse,
Fell on deaf ears helping the undertaker and the driver of the hearse.

The virus seen as a problem on someone else's plate,
The observers calling it bad luck or just fate.
Brought on by a trip to the beach, a protest, or just a night on the town,
Social disobedience resulted in the cases not going down.

Why have we become so disconnected?
So little empathy for those sick, dying and the families affected.
Call it a political affliction or gamblers just playing the odds,
The statistical outcome relied on by Sweden, initiated by some Scandinavian Gods.

We are all caught between a hard place and a rock,
Failing to social distance, is more than just talk.
We all have a moral duty not to spread the disease,
Our nation needs to see the forest, and not forget some of the trees.

"COVID-19 IS BACK WITH A VENGENCE"

"COVID HAS HARROWING COMPLICATIONS"

-The Wall Street Journal
June 12th, 2020

WALL STREET BLUES

The investment world runs on risk and reward,
Like freedom hinges often on the use of a dove or a sword.
The gears of progress recently came to a halt,
Losses have mounted, Coronavirus was the party at fault.

Now restarted, the country making money once more,
The brokers on Wall Street again keeping score.
Now with cases increasing at a record pace,
A major market adjustment down, brings on a Wall Street sad face.

The risks of opening up offset by lost lives,
The relief to the problem achieved when the cure arrives.
Betting on the over and under when that will be,
Billions at stake, the price for a cure definitely not free.

In one of the biggest gambles in one hundred years,
The top one percent want to shift into the highest gears.
Will it be a home run, or the Wall Street Blues?
A vaccine in the Fall, will be a grand slam, and be the biggest news.

"GOVENOR LEE DISCUSSES FACE MASKS"

"VOUNTEERS REQUESTED FOR VACCINE STUDY"

-The Knoxville Central
June 13th, 2020

WHAT DAY IS IT?

As the self-quarantine restrictions rage on,
The events of significance are now gone.
No adventure or entertainment with a big group,
Morning, afternoon, evening repeating in an endless loop.

Everyday seems the same, just to stay safe,
The hazards of the virus lurk, going out seems unsafe.
Losing track of yesterday, and the day before,
Wondering about August, what is in store?

Beaches open, maybe the movie theatre,
and the zoo,
Masks required, social distancing too.
Tired of television, read too many books,
Now cleaning, shopping and one of the designated cooks.

So difficult to grasp the reality of it all,
Hoping for sports to be played, in the late summer and fall.
Each day I arise, wondering what day it is,
My brain now numbed; I have to admit.

"SINGLE DAY RECORD BROKEN WITH 3,822 INFECTIONS"

"75% OF ICU BEDS FILLED"

-Tampa Bay Times
June 15th, 2020

WHAT'S AHEAD?

When COVID-19 says goodbye to all,
We realize the world has changed, no trips to the mall.
Staying away from any sick or threatening person,
Avoiding any opportunity for things to worsen.

Telecommuting for work or a doctor's appointment,
Definitely tomorrow is here, not a big disappointment.
No subways, traffic jams or long commutes,
Avoiding others, no need for personal disputes.

No one will call me excessive or a freak,
When I Purell my house, a new antiseptic technique.
Gloves and a mask on when I am around others,
That is everyone, except my wife, kids, and brothers.

Maybe it is just mental or just safe practice,
Or not doing using a mask and gloves will be called malpractice.
The good old days of yesterday are gone,
All we need is Mr. Clean to sing his advertising song.

"WILD ANTELOPE HUNT
CANCELLED FOR CHARITY"

"1.85 MILLION DOLLARS
ALLOCATED TO COVID RELIEF"

-The Omaha World Herald
June 17th, 2020

WHAT COULD HAVE BEEN

Turning back the clock just 180 days,
Memories of those days lost in the haze.
The news from China of a new viral disease,
The outbreak in Wuhan, started by a bat eating Chinese.

The outbreak sounded so surreal, like it was just a myth,
Yet China locked down with global notice forthwith.
Like a pandemic bomb, people would scatter,
To fifty countries by air, the world leaders thought it would not matter.

Country by country waited to close-down,
As the virus infected thousands, putting so many in the ground.
If those in China that were sick had just stayed put,
The Pandemic would have ended, the global economy would not have gone caput.

What could have been, if we had understood,
Shutting down, locking doors, all would have been good.
The lives of so many now are forever lost,
Failure to close-down, has come with a terrible cost.

"INDOOR DINING HALTED AT RESTAURANTS"

"BARS AND GYMS ORDERED TO CLOSE"

-The Los Angeles Times
June 29th, 2020

FEELS LIKE A DREAM

Shut in, now on my one hundred twelfth day,
Like a fictitious virtual reality, seems like a Tennessee Williams play.
The words of Willie Loman, echo in my head,
Too crazy to explain, like "How fast has the virus has spread".

After my fifth cup of coffee the cobwebs clear,
Going out for groceries, a necessity, the virus, I fear.
I pretend to be a super-hero, just like one of the X-Men,
With a mask on my face, a disguise, it is easy to pretend.

Fighting a nearly invisible enemy, seems impossible,
Yet, the arrival of a vaccine will make it possible.
The world is being tested like never before,
In a fight for survival, the jury is still out on what is in store.

I am waiting to wake up from this bad dream,
Anxious to be in a crowd, back in the mainstream.
For the time being I just have to carry on,
I have added a cape to my outfit, until the pandemic is gone.

"INDOOR DINING HALTED AT RESTAURANTS"

"BARS AND GYMS ORDERED TO CLOSE"

-The Miami Herald
July 1st, 2020

LOCKED DOWN AGAIN

Like the Black Outs of World War Two,
Overbearing restrictions on society are once again true,
No more sit-down restaurants, bars, and ocean beaches,
The lock down back in place, to protect and stop the virus's reaches.

The "stay at home" mandate now the law,
Violators will be arrested, the surge of cases, the final straw.
Governors now taking drastic steps, to stop the virus's spread,
Trying to reduce the numbers of the sick and dead.

Young adult ignoring the wear mask rules,
Their disregard of social distancing, an act of fools.
So many think the virus is a hoax,
Yet, the rise in cases and deaths, terrorize the older folks.

We are counting on the Governors to stop this threat,
When this crisis will end is a long shot bet,
Smart money is dedicated to stay healthy and safe,
This insane social isolation is our only fail-safe.

"INDOOR DINING HALTED AT RESTAURANTS"

"BARS AND GYMS ORDERED TO CLOSE"

-The St. Louis Tribune
July 6th, 2020

MIXED MESSAGES

The truth about the Coronavirus, often is skewed,
The CDC and the White House are engaged in a media feud.
The number of confirmed cases, and those that die,
Are real numbers, that leave thousands to cry,

The CDC announcing that with thousands out in mass,
Causing confirmed cases to soar, many more will pass.
Yet, the White House announced 99% will not get sick,
The danger of this contagious virus just a dirty trick.

The truth from Dr. Fauci is, "We're in terrible shape!",
With so many violating social restrictions, a national disgrace.
The pandemic has set us back weeks and weeks,
It will not be safe to go out until the virus peaks.

The future of the country is uncertain on so many levels,
The growing scourge could be controlled by devils.
Hoping and praying that Our Almighty Lord,
Helps us launch a virus free world, with as many possible on board.

"YOUTH STRICKEN BY COVID IN MISSOURI"

"CAMP KANKUK REPORTS 82 KIDS TEST POSITIVE"

-The Columbia News Tribune
July 10th, 2020

A DAY AT CAMP

The parents that like to gamble with the lives of their kids,
Send them to summer camp, which the CDC now forbids.
Hiking, Swimming, Boating with others,
Bringing home the virus to their grandmothers.

It is madness to think that going to camp is worth the risk,
With the number of cases rising, the contagiousness so brisk.
Fake news on the TV, reporting it is safe to mingle,
The consequences awaiting, a hospital bed, that is a single.

For the kids that dodge the virus, and do not get sick,
The ones that do not dodge it, are victims of a dirty trick.
What camp counselor with brains, condones this plan?
Putting at risk, little tykes pretending to be Batman.

The madness of carrying on like everything is okay,
Illness, ventilators, lives in peril, presently come into play.
 Negligent not to protect the kids we love,
A day at camp, insanity, we have never dreamed of.

"MILLIONS PULLED BACK INTO POVERTY BY COVID"

"DATA SUGGESTS COVID STILL ACTIVE IN NEW YORK"

-The New York Times
July 11th, 2020

PANDEMIC HALLUCINATIONS

The passage of time, shut up in your house,
Hallucinations occurring, like dropping LSD with Mickey Mouse.
The White Rabbit keeps saying, "Feed Your Head",
The Grim reaper is there, asking, "Do you want to be dead?"

All these crazy dreams brought on by the virus this year,
Looking for any good news, a sports team to cheer.
Church on Zoom is just not the same,
Isolation the cause, no one to blame.

The lack of mental stimulation brings on bad dreams,
The continuation of the pandemic, one of many dreamt extremes.
Eating macaroni another, just five days a week,
A nightmare that would cause anyone to freak.

Without the day to day contact with friends,
The walls close in, each day seems like it never ends.
It is unbelievable that we are stuck in this place,
Tomorrow so near, hoping the virus does an "about face".

"TRUMP IRKED AT DR. BRIX FOR HER STATEMENTS"

"NEW COVID TESTS-WHERE ARE THEY?"

-USA Today
July 12th, 2020

WHAT WENT WRONG?

As the Coronavirus cases continue to rise,
The number of elderly deaths is no surprise.
After all, Covid-19 is not like the flu,
More like SARS or MERS, but most say who knew.

Those between 21 and 39, at the beach or in the bars,
Not too concerned about getting sick, self-proclaimed stars.
The young populace so selfish and unconcerned,
Believing there bulletproof, lifetime lessons to be learned.

Infecting others, the young folks feel no shame,
Their sense of moral responsibility, definitely the blame.
The only course of correction, strict rules in place,
The goal, to save the lives of innocents, no disgrace.

It is not too late to right this ship,
Everyone under forty must get a grip.
An understanding of community needed to take sensible actions,
Will bring us together for a future crisis, hopefully with no stupid distractions.

"I'M NOT MISLEADING THE PUBLIC" – DR. ANTHONY FAUCI

"WHITE HOUSE DENIES FIRING DR. FAUCI"

-The Los Angeles Times
July 13th, 2020

DR. FAUCI FIRED?

The reality show on tv that we see today,
A public health hurricane that is blowing us away.
If the number of cases were measured in wind speed,
It would be a Category 4, an emergency decreed.

The confusion created by the news from the White House,
They say, "Mild breezes today, no reason to grouse."
Dr. Fauci's forecast is much different,
Ninety mile an hour gale, do not be indifferent.

The President so upset at the weather predicted,
He fired Dr. Fauci, the result of being so conflicted.
The nation now shocked at his insane action,
The weather so obvious, his termination a meteorological infraction.

As we move forward sheltered and masked,
Our goal is to stay well, everyone tasked.
The news media should air Dr. Fauci's reports,
Maybe the only way to survive, a gesture of last resorts.

"VENTILATER USE REACHES AND ALL TIME HIGH"

"3,910 NEW COVID-19 CASES REPORTED"

-The Arizona Republic
July 14th, 2020

LOCKED UP AGAIN

Four and one-half months under the Coronavirus spell,
No One has answers that I can tell.
Florida, Arizona, and Texas, exploding with cases,
Some folks in those states without social graces.

California's youth again out of control,
At the beach, or in the bar dancing to rock and roll.
The Governor left with no choice but to lock down,
Protecting seniors, turning each city into a ghost town.

The dichotomy between money and health,
Choosing life for some, at the expense of others wealth.
The greatest economy in life he whole world,
Partially shut down, no flags furled.

The good of society left to the men at the top,
ICU's and hospital beds filled; cases need to stop.
It is worked around the world when things were shut down,
Pray to God it works this time, so went go back downtown.

"MIAMI-DADE COVID CASES TOP 101,000"

"100 DEATHS REPORTED FIVE DAYS IN A ROW"

-The Miami Herald
July 15th, 2020

A HOAX IT IS NOT

Anytime the word "hoax" is used, consider who said it,
Fact checking needed, all would admit.
A "Hoax" is a play to confuse or deceive,
An alternative reality that someone wants you to believe.

The President declared the virus was a hoax,
Now 174 days later, there are 140,000 dead folks.
Obviously, the pandemic is a national crisis,
More serious than the medical process
zymolsis.

We are waiting for a vaccine, to save the day,
Each new morning hoping that all will be okay.
As we ponder a few more months locked in,
It is obvious that our new best friends will be scotch,
vodka and gin.

Whatever the motivation not to take the virus serious,
It has turned into a scandal, so mysterious.
So many now seeing the foolishness of it all,
Will it cause a national political change in the USA in late Fall?

"COVID CASES UP, BUT THINGS ARE IMPROVING"

"VACCINE TRIALS COMMENCE - 1,000 SIGN UP"

-The San Diego Union Times
July 15th, 2020

SAYING NO TO MASKS

As the Pandemic grows each day,
The CDC's guidelines say wearing a mask, stopping the virus, it is the only way.
In some states the protesters say, "Hell No".
In those states the contagion does not slow.

Citing some absolute Constitutional right,
Not wearing a mask, getting Covid-19, not too bright.
In this national crisis, a real need to stop the virus's spread,
Wearing a mask will reduce the number of sick and dead.

The extremes between us, keep getting wider,
What is for the good of the order gets lost, politics the divider.
Time to get serious, all need to comply with the health rules,
Those that claim virility for going mask less, are real fools.

There is no justification for infecting others,
Especially if their someone's brothers, sisters, or mothers.
Bringing everyone together for the country's good,
Respecting the rule of law, righteousness and civility understood.

"COVID-19 DEATHS SURGE IN GEORGIA"

"GEORGIA'S HOSPITALS GROAN UNDER ASSAULT OF CASES"

-Atlanta Journal Constitution
July 18th, 2020

REAL OR NOT REAL

The Corona 19 Virus has taken center stage,
Masks, covering faces, required, not the rage.
The fake news spreading that the virus is a hoax,
Disbelief that it is serious, some telling jokes.

How can the reality of this threat?
Be total ignored, like there was nothing to sweat.
Medical science confirms Covid-19 lasts for years,
Side effects could be serious, bringing lots of fears.

The bottom line to this incredible fraud,
Lives are being lost; the entire health system flawed.
The need for everyone to wake up,
Getting rid of Covid-19, so critical, we can never to give up.

Correcting misconceptions is going to take time,
There will be more lives lost, should be a crime.
Freedom in America does not include being ill-conceived,
The truth about the virus, must be told, and hopefully believed.

"IT'S 'CRUNCH TIME' FOR A COVID-19 VACCINE" – DR. ANTHONY FAUCI

"MISSOULIAN'S ARE CONFUSED ON MASK RULES"

           -The Missoulian
              July 19th, 2020

THE VACCINE

Not since Dr. Jonas Salk developed a cure for polio,
Has the world awaited a vaccine, hoping the virus's spread to slow.
Now as we approach the end five months of fear,
The promise of a vaccine awaits, maybe the miracle of the year.

Virologists have been working night and day,
To kill the virus so deadly in every way.
Trials have been expanded, looking for side effects,
Weighing the positives, ending the sending of last respects.

Billions of people, globally, have been put at risk,
In the Pandemic of 2020, the infections spread so brisk.
As so many people failed to comply with social distancing,
The result now, most sheltered at home, using air conditioning.

What will happen when the vaccine is given,
Will those that refuse the shot, be ultimately forgiven.
Whatever happens the vaccine will bring great change,
And the end of a year that has been stranger than strange.

"PRITZKER OPENS DOOR FOR FINES FOR NOT WEARING A MASK"

"STAYING CALM IS THE KEY TO BEING HAPPY STAYING AT HOME"

-The Chicago Tribune
July 24th, 2020

THE STATUS QUO

When we rise to face the challenges of each day,
The news on TV paints a grim picture, the virus at play.
Those that challenged the restrictions are paying now,
Praying for survival, and banking on advanced medical know-how.

It is impossible to understand why so many went to the beach,
Perhaps thinking that the ocean breezes would make the virus out of reach.
California and Florida, now seeing the results of this folly,
Doctors and nurses, trying to save lives, it is not fun or jolly.

Dr. Fauci amazed at the contagiousness and spread of this virus,
Now so many cases, four million now asking "why us?"
The US leading the world in cases reported,
The White House distressed, saying the numbers are unsupported.

The drama continues, as we remain sheltered in,
So many saying the pandemic is a hoax, a mortal sin.
Just accepting the status quo, for all to stay living and well,
The bottom line to this story, stay safe to avoid the heavenly farewell.

"NEW MEXICO JAILS FILED WITH COVID-19 INMATES"

"16,000 CASES REPORTED IN NEW MEXICO"

-The Albuquerque Lobo
July 26th, 2020

STAYING THE COURSE

The public restrictions that appear from the county seat,
Hated by all, so voluminous, reading them a feat.
The message always the same, keep people apart,
Social distancing required, staying well the goal,
for those that are smart.

Only a few times in two hundred years,
Has a national edict brought so much fear.
In 1918 during the last months of World War One,
The influenza pandemic had just begun.

The science of virology was so elementary and new,
The H1N1 virus was deadly, and the doctors treating, had not a clue.
One hundred years later, a microbe just as dangerous, has us on the run,
Looking for a vaccine to end it and be done.

We are just as vulnerable as we were way back when,
Saving our loved ones, whether women or men,
The only way to end this apocalyptic force,
Stay at home, stay safe, "stay the course".

"1,278 HOSPITALIZED AS COVID-19 SPREADS"

"TEENS AND YOUNG ADULTS GATHER AND SPREAD VIRUS"

-The Phoenix Republic
July 28th, 2020

SORRY ISN'T ENOUGH

In this time when anyone can get sick,
Drinking at a bar, too close, turns out to be a dirty trick.
A couple weeks later. symptoms just appear,
With no cure or vaccine, the virus can get severe.

Cases start with a few that are out of line,
Then some exposed cannot breathe, a serious sign.
At the hospital, Intubated, then on a ventilator,
Family then praying for their recovery, to our creator.

It is a vicious cycle that just repeats,
When patients' die, the result, lost heart beats.
Those that started the spread, often recover,
Not knowing the damage caused, consciences may go undercover.

No words can replace the loss of a loved one,
The virus with no cure, cannot be undone.
Even realizing the damage, an apology so tough,
Saying you are sorry after the fact, is never enough.

"ALASKA AIRLINES MANDATES MASKS ON ALL FLIGHTS"

"GOVENOR JAY INSLEE RE-INSTITUTES COVID-19 RESPRICTIONS"

-The Tacoma News Tribune
July 29th, 2020

STAY WORRY FREE

Time to de-stress, no worries ahead,
Years of life left, nothing to dread.
News each day on the public health threat,
A media barrage, trying to change your mindset.

It is time to focus on your diversion of choice,
A song to sing, a challenge to your voice,
Find a musical instrument to play,
The performance complete, get ready for Broadway.

Pick up a paint brush, pretend you are Monet,
Paint a masterpiece, put it on display.
A great novel is just a keystroke away,
Do not fret the critics, they will not have the final say.

Open your mind to things off the charts,
Enable brilliance released, a cornucopia of smarts.
Time is precious, live life with glee,
Whatever happens, try to stay worry free.

"MINNESOTA PASSES ONE HUNDRED THOUSAND CASES"

"157 HOSPITALIZED THIS WEEK WITH COVID 19"

-Minneapolis Star Tribune
July 29th, 2020

HAPPY IS THE WAY

We are in this Pandemic for the long haul,
Social distancing, Wearing a mask, each person's duty, and call.
The rollercoaster of life, has its ups and downs,
The ride always bumpier if you are wearing a frown.

So, let us try to be happy on each sunny day,
Find things to do, to help others, along the way.
Be supportive of family during these tough times,
Make each day peaches and cream, not lemons and limes.

Look towards the future, when a vaccine is in place,
Until then, planning for tomorrow, may require a different pace.
Slowing down each day, to smell the roses,
Requires all to listen to health officials, masks over everyone's noses.

There is no solution or cure for this pandemic,
But staying healthy and safe requires a plan that is systemic.
Staying upbeat and positive will pave the way,
Until we are free of this virus, and we can once again go out and play.

"DR. STELLA IMMANUEL TOUTS HYDROXYCLOROQUINE AS CURE FOR COVID 19"

"DR. STELLA FIGHTS DEMONS IN MOUNTAIN OF FIRE AND MIRACLES MINISTRY"

TRUMP POSTS VIDEO OF DR. STELLA, AND CALLS HER HIS FAVORITE DOCTOR"

-Houston Chronicle
July 30th, 2020

HOW WEIRD CAN IT GET?

This week, the Coronavirus's source, a new theory disclosed,
A Texas' nurse's claims went viral, her craziness exposed.
She said the virus was brought by aliens from outer space,
Their astral UFO's were sent to earth, to set up an aerial base.

Even stranger were her claims of sex with them,
Her lies and fantasies, meant to cause mass mayhem.
The President announcing that he believed her claims,
He said, Hydroxychloroquine the cure, obviously he is playing her mind games.

This madness surfacing, intended to cause more fear,
The only answer, a preventative vaccine for the virus needed, by the end of the year.
Dr. Stella, a mysterious figure, that appeared out of nowhere,
Her news conference staged, at the Supreme Court, it could have been anywhere.

Someone said, "I feel like I'm in the Twilight Zone",
Rod Serling defined it, "A place between science and superstition, that is totally unknown".
Trying to find reason and logic, a goal for the next "Mission Impossible".
We need to flip this switch from "On to Off", to escape and find what is possible.

"YOUTH CASES EXPLODE"

"MASKS REJECTED BY TEENS AND YOUNG ADULTS"

-Orlando Sentinel
August 1st, 2020

THE TRUTH ABOUT MASKS

There are moments of truth in these Pandemic days,
The resonance of reality hits us in so many ways.
Herman Cain, a famous CEO, did not wear a mask,
The Corona virus reacted to his indifference, took him to task.

It now appears that the CDC has not lied about preventive measures,
Wearing a mask preserves your health, one of your greatest treasures.
Dr.'s Fauci and Brix are the speakers of truth,
They are the scientists, each one a virus sleuth.

It is a fact, that wearing a mask, will stop the virus's spread,
It will reduce the numbers of sick and dead.
Yet, there are some that say no to the mask,
Policing the violators is an impossible task.

So here we are facing more months shut down,
The lives of so many at risk in every town.
The harsh reality of this terrible pandemic,
Not wearing a mask will spread a virus that is so systemic.

"COVID 19 CASES SURGING IN CHILDREN AND TEENS"

"STATE'S COVID-19 CASES REACH 574,411"

-The Los Angeles Times
August 2nd, 2020

FAILURE TO PITCH IN

History will tell the story, of those who were selfish and defied,
They failed to social distant, wearing masks was not even tried.
During this pandemic most them were under thirty,
The Covid cases and deaths they failed to see.

When Dr. Fauci called for everyone to pitch in,
Urging all to stay at home, the young adults said it was just media spin.
Believing the White House's drivel that the virus was not bad,
They went out to party, spreading the virus, so sad.

Now California, Florida, Texas, and Arizona are locked down,
The virus cases caused from beach goers or partiers downtown.
This social irresponsibility must be corrected,
Before thousands of others get infected.

The powers that be, can act, to change this course,
Sensitivity retraining, a media barrage, more social intercourse.
This new normal has put so much out of control,
We need to regroup to continue our nation's roll.

"WEARING MASKS WORKS"

"STATE COVID 19 CASES REACH 102,130"

-The State Newspaper
(Columbia, SC)
August 12th, 2020

FROZEN IN TIME

The world it seems has been frozen in place,
The Coronavirus spreading, at a ridiculous pace.
Everyone sheltering, staying away from others,
The energy of life, sucked out, as the virus smothers.

Schools try to open, teachers worried about get sick,
Parents saying home school impossible, teaching English and Arithmetic.
Millions out of work, businesses closed, too much grief,
Hard not to worry, no solutions at hand, or relief.

Groundhog Day seems to have become a reality,
The end of the year may bring the pandemic's finality.
We are trying our best to carry on with life,
The obstacles mounting, bringing increasing strife.

With very little moving, we are anxious but still optimistic,
That the vaccine being developed will be synergistic.
Until then we will stay in what seems, "Frozen in Time"
During this inconceivable pandemic, happening hopefully, only once in a lifetime.

CDC COVID-19 GUIDELINES

- ALWAYS STAY SIX FEET APART

- STAY HOME

- AVOID LARGE GATHERINGS

- DON'T TOUCH SURFACES

- AVOID SHAKING HANDS

- WASH HANDS/DISINFECT

Author's Acknowledgements
• • •

The inspiration for this book of pandemic poems came for being shut in for weeks and weeks. The new reality brought on by the pandemic has changed America. No one knows what the future will bring, and how we will work, play, and interact with others.

Always with the inspiration from my wife, Marylynn, and my son, A.J. and his family, my sister-in-law, Sally Rygmyr, and my friends, Ralph and Susan Erickson, John and Colleen Crawford, Les Widerynski, Rick Stohr, and Hon. John M. Meyer I have continued to write poems. I have also sought confirmation of the quality of the poems by sending them to these friends for their critique and response.

Through the collective efforts of all the above-named individuals and the gift of spontaneously writing these poems, with the help of the Lord, this poem book came to be. I give thanks for the opportunity to present these poetic verses to the world.

JPK

Author's Biography
•••

Jim Kintner, lawyer/poet/author, has previously written "Scottish Links- A Pilgrimage to Scotland", "Swinging in Rhyme", "Poems from Heaven", Volumes One and Two, "La Courtine – A Surgeon's Memoir", "The 52nd Fighter Group", and now presents "Pandemic Poems of 2020". After a long career as a tax lawyer, Mr. Kintner has found in his retirement time to write books and poetry. He lives with his wife, Marylynn, and his dog, Lucy, in Indio, California.

www.ingramcontent.com/pod-product-compliance
Lightning Source LLC
Chambersburg PA
CBHW051406290426
44108CB00015B/2168